CW00601759

Sh
RATTLE
& Custard!

by
Martin Brown

With grateful acknowledgement to
Colin (Sam) Baxter,
esteemed artist, guitarist, and computer whiz.

Author's Note:
Many of these poems have featured in
the Coventry Telegraph.
Some of them have won prizes in poetry competitions.
Others have just lain around,
stubbornly refusing to earn their keep.

Until now.

CONTENTS

This poem's not been tested on animals…

This poem's not been tested on animals
I refused to read it out to my cat,
Not since I read him my sonnet
And he turned round and showed me his back.

This poem is an organic product,
Sustainably sourced from my brain.
This poem is completely recyclable,
You can read it again and again.

This poem is carbon neutral
In a Switzerland sort of way.
To save on electric consumption
It's best read during the day.

This poem is eco-friendly,
It's non-polluting, and clean.
The more you keep reading this poem
The more you can feel a bit green.

Animal Rights

Stroppy bees stop making honey
Until they're given pots of money.

Mice demand appearance fees,
Turn their noses up at cheese.

Swans complain they cannot talk,
Fish decide they want to walk.

Rats all sue for defamation,
Amoeba call for sex education.

Owls refuse to fly at nights:
That's what you get with animal rights.

The Car Park

We took our car to a car park
We thought it deserved a treat.
But all that was there, were lines of cars
All parked in rows, so neat.

No swings, no slides, no vehicle rides
Not even a motorised zoo.
No drive-in picnic or vehicular golf
Nothing, in short, to do.

We'd had to queue for a ticket
And then, it started to rain.
So we all drove home, disappointed.
We won't be going again.

Strings

Britain's secured by strings
- there must be ten thousand or more -
All tied to big metal rings
That are glued to the ocean floor.

Beware The Long Fingered Octopus!
Or The Squid With The Slithery Arm!
Neither of these are friendly to us,
And may do us unspeakable harm!

By untying each string
They could set us afloat,
Adrift on the sea,
Like a rudderless boat!

That's why we have a Navy, you see,
With frigates, and subs, and military things,
To make sure we're safe in this big choppy sea,
By keeping an eye on those thousands of strings.

The Bread Tree

When the Bread Tree sheds its loaves,
they tumble to the ground.
The Hungry hear them falling
and rush from miles around.

They gather up the slices
- it's rare such food is free –
then carry off their bounty,
to the nearby Butter Tree.

There they tap the churned-up sap,
to spread with home-made knives.
Through the meagre winter months
this helps sustain their lives.

Cyclists

There's a one-legged unicyclist
who pedals into town!
His leg goes like a clapper
as his wheel goes round and round!

There's lots of two-legged bicyclists,
- they're as common as muck.
Seeing three, or more, of them
won't bring you extra luck.

You're guaranteed good fortune, though,
- as sure as eggs is eggs -
if you spot a lucky tricycle
whose rider has three legs.

Debate

The well-dressed man declared to all:
Everything's just fine!
Our universe is guided by
Intelligent design!

I said: *They're just two words for God,*
And he does not exist!
The man fixed me with narrowed eyes -
Down came the scarlet mist.

Prove He don't exist! he yelled.
Prove so! I answered back.
I'll prove He does! he snarled at me,
Then leapt into attack.

We kicked and clawed and wrestled,
A mean and vicious fight.
Tearing clothes and drawing blood,
To prove which one was right.

In the end, I knocked him out,
Which made me right, I guess.
Though, God or no, I only know
Our world is sure a mess.

Friendly Fire

I'm the Health and Safety Officer
For the Boys on our front line,
Who call me (quite affectionately)
An interfering swine.

I ask for risk assessments
Each time they fire a gun
And a full report on hazards
Before a battle's won.

But now I'm in the medics' tent,
In circumstances dire.
With a bullet up my fundament:
They call it *friendly fire.*

Me and God

Me and God, we're best of mates,
We often have a chat.
When people ask me - what about?
I tell them… this, and that.

When we were young, we used to play
War games, in his den.
When he was glum, to cheer him up,
I'd let him win, just now and then.

Lately, though, we sit and talk,
And put the world to rights.
We'll often lose all track of time,
And jaw for days and nights.

Blasphemers always make him sigh,
And atheists as well.
Just wait, I'll say, until they die,
Then send them straight to Hell!

And what of great disasters,
That re-occur through history?
Just leave alone, I say to God,
They help to give you mystery.

And still, at times, it gets him down,
He wants to leave, break free.
Any time, I say to him,
Just give the job to me!

Yes, Me and God, we're best of mates,
We often sit and chat.
And who am I? Old Nick, of course!
I thought you'd gathered that!

Orion's Belt

When things all get on top of me
And life is one long sigh,
It's soothing in the dark to see
Orion's Belt up in the sky.

But then, the panic hits me!
What if that Belt were gone?
Orion's Pants would surely fall
And smother everyone!

And that's why I'm appealing
For cash to put things right:
To send some giant braces up
Into the starlit night

And help make sure Orion's Pants
Stay firmly in their place,
Held by Belt and Braces
Safely up in space.

Slug

I taught a slug to fly today.
I gave it wings, it soared away.

Flew somersaults and loop the loops,
Figure eights and daring swoops.

Leaving after, every time,
A heavenly trail of aerial slime.

Not too good for birds, I fear,
With hindsight, not a good idea.

But gently, then, the slug touched down,
And said that it preferred the ground:

I feel much safer with the ants,
Clouds are fine, but I like plants.

Thanks for the wings, but, for getting around,
I'd rather crawl along the ground!

And off he slimed, and that was that;
Ungrateful wretch! - I squashed him flat!

Sweet Dreams

I was lying in a crinkly bag,
when, much to my alarm,
a jelly baby peered inside
and grabbed me by the arm!

It pulled me up from out the bag,
and with a sickly sound,
dipped me in a sugar bowl,
and passed me all around
some gaudy, coloured substances
of every size and shape;
I screamed - oh, how I shouted out,
and struggled to escape!

I sensed my captors laughing
at my feeble little squeals,
and shivered as I heard them say
He now knows how it feels
to be handled and selected
as a tiny sugared treat,
and kept inside a goodie bag,
as something nice to eat!

I found myself being lifted up
and stuffed down deep inside
the gullet of a lemon drop,
and felt that I'd just died!
I woke up in a heavy sweat,
as one about to scream,
confiding in my loving wife,
I told her of my dream.

I was hoping for some sympathy,
but she just yawned and said:
Don't eat so many sweets, you fool,
before you come to bed!

My Dog, The Musician

My dog likes to play the piano,
He keeps me awake every night.
He's practiced since he was a puppy,
But still he just can't get it right.

He's soft and he's friendly and harmless,
Since he lost all his teeth in a fight.
Any pain is produced by his playing,
For his Bach is much worse than his bite.

When I'm Bored

When I'm bored, my brain stagnates,
My mind packs up and then migrates
To other places far and wide,
Where things of interest may reside:

Like clouds that giggle, laugh and joke
And proposition wisps of smoke,
Where charming snakes eat prey with spoons
And frogs carve slogans on balloons.

Where mountains droop and sleep at night,
Then yawn and stretch in morning light.
And mice are busy ironing sheets
While friendly wardrobes roam the streets.

Then when I've had enough of these:
Of buttered clocks and walking cheese,
And fluffy mud and talking beer,
My mind returns, refreshed and clear,

Back to the world of grey and rain,
Ready to be bored again.

Umbrella Head

I come from the planet Lotzarain,
the peculiar creature said.
My real name is 'Putyabroliup'
but my friends call me Umbrella Head.

Then, as the heavens opened,
his head did just the same.
So I huddled close beneath it,
sheltering from the rain.

Shake, Rattle and Custard

My aunt was a Bill Haley lookalike,
(Far stranger things have been known).
She'd tour with a rock'n'roll outfit,
Rather than staying at home.

With her kiss curl and puckered up lips,
Her raucous and gravely voice,
Low slung guitar round her hips,
She was the rocker of choice.

My uncle was taken aback,
Initially baffled and flustered,
By messages stuck up with blu tac,
Like *Make your own gravy and custard-*

I'm too busy rolling and rocking,
To spend my time doing your tea,
So you'll have to start learning some cooking
It's the rock'n'roll lifestyle for me!

My uncle was all of a rage,
In fact, he was frankly disgusted,
That his wife was cavorting on stage,
While he was left making the custard.

Arguments followed, and then they split up,
Divorcing the following summer.
My uncle hitched up with a pastry cook,
While aunty married a drummer.

Years later, they're both very happy:
My uncle has lots of home baking,
And my aunt is still belting out rock'n'roll hits,
Rattling and rolling and shaking.

A Visit from God

God appeared at my bedside, last week,
I'd hoped for some much-needed rest.
But, like a bad ache, He kept me awake:
Boy! That God was a pest!

He was fully prepared, with a long questionnaire,
He claimed it was 'market research'.
Did I think that a prayer could be made anywhere
Or were they heard best in a church?

He asked what I thought about sinning
And my views about life after death.
And heaven and hell, and much more as well
With scarcely a pause to draw breath.

Did I think all religions were valid?
And all beliefs really the same?
Were all great disasters just natural?
Or should we seek someone to blame?

And how many angels can dance
On a pinhead at any one time?
Could I think up some brand new commandments?
Should blasphemy still be a crime?

At last, He announced; *Nearly finished!*
The very last one on My list!
Now answer me true, I beg you please do;
Do you think that I really exist?

My mind was a state, I was barely awake,
All I could think was, *Please, go.*
I was in a foul mood, I knew it was rude,
When I turned round and shouted out *No!*

I'm afraid that He looked rather startled
And with barely a moment to spare,
Like a pantomime joke, in a brief puff of smoke,
He disappeared into thin air.

I puzzled at this for a moment,
For I've never been one to think deep.
I gave a brief shrug, my blankets a tug,
And straight away went off to sleep.

About a Dog

There is a dog that loves to yap
Enough to make your patience snap.
Every day it gets let out
And yaps and yaps and runs about.
It yaps at birds, it yaps at cats,
It yaps at people walking past.
It yaps at wind, it yaps at rain,
It yaps because it has no brain.
Its owners sometime go away
And leave it out to yap all day.
It yaps at clouds, it yaps at planes,
It yaps when people call it names.
It's yapping now - oh! flippin' heck!
I'd like to wring its yapping neck!

The Astronaut's Day Off

Mooching around on an unexplored planet,
cooling excitement to well off the boil.
Determined to miss any useful discovery,
shunning, on purpose, interesting soil.

Spending some time with some old magazines,
idly thumbing, and stifling a yawn.
Ignoring the rise of the secondary sun
latticing shadows on an alien dawn.

Avoiding, today, those unexplained caverns
where challenge and mystery patiently lurk.
Instead, thinking beer, and giving a sigh:
just a few hours, and then back to work.

Cats in Masks…

Cats in masks buy stolen honey
in sugar crates, with wooden money,
from shady mice who borrow towels
and mortar boards to hoodwink owls.
While counterfeit biologists are circulating blood,
falsely elongated ghosts are busy burning mud.
Paper-mâchè fishing boats chase aquatic sheep,
surfing on my brainwaves while I lie fast asleep.

22nd Century Child

I love to hear
     my grandma talk
of how, when young,
     she used to walk
through woods, up hills,
     - that sort of place –
before the world
     ran out of space.

My thinking cap

I had a thinking cap
That thought a bit too well.
When I put it on my head
My brain began to swell:

I wrestled with equations,
And the cause of earthly strife,
The origins of the universe
And the futility of life.
And whether there was a meaning
To every single dream,
And if our latest manager
Could build a decent team.

Do we have free will
Or are we led by fate?
Why, whenever we need one
Are the buses always late?
How bad is global warming?
What caused the credit crunch?
Has mankind got a future?
How fattening is my lunch?

Sparks shot out my cranium!
Smoke poured out my ears!
My thinking cap was working -
Beyond my wildest fears!
Hastily, I pulled it off
And stuffed it in a drawer,
Locked it up and vowed I wouldn't
Use it any more.

Instead, I'd face in ignorance,
The questions of existence,
Confront them with a blissful smile,
Without my cap's assistance.

My Tortoise

My tortoise likes playing the drums,
But his beat is tremendously slow.
Give him a drumstick to hold in his mouth
And tap, tap, tap, he'll go.

I fixed him a job with a chart-topping group,
But I knew it unlikely to last.
The high hat and snare stayed out of his reach,
And the tunes that they played were too fast.

They speeded him up on recordings
But touring, he found out, was hell.
When fans started screaming at concerts
He'd simply shrink back in his shell.

The end finally came in the winter,
On a planned Christmas tour of the nation.
My tortoise instead, just took to his bed,
And went into deep hibernation.

He's happier now, back here at home,
Though fortune and fame have both fled.
When Springtime arrives, I know he's alive,
When I hear a *tap, tap,* in the shed.

Lost and Found

The lady stood up:
I've lost my lap!
Her partner groaned
At this latest mishap.

I had it just now!
Please look all around!
It can't have gone far,
It must be found!

He peered under the table
Looked under the chairs
Went out in the hall
And searched up the stairs.

He checked in the fridge
By the yoghurt and cream.
But the lap, it appeared,
Was nowhere to be seen.

Without my lap
Life won't be the same!
She sobbed, and sat down,
And found it again.

Nestco.

Being the first,
he'd cornered the market
in ready-made nests
for selling to birds.
Nestco, of course!
he'd shout, pointing up
to a mock-twig confection
embossed with those words.

Freed from the humdrum
of gathering bits,
birds put on weight,
grew fond of the ground.
Found time to argue,
fall out with their partners:
it's hardly surprising
if numbers are down.

The Cold Catcher

I know a man who catches colds
And puts them in a tin.
When this is full he empties it
Into a larger bin.

From there they're taken to a room
That's warm and not too dry:
Just the right conditions so
The germs can multiply.

When there's lots they're taken out
And gaily flung around
To get up all the noses of
The people in the town

Who cough and spread, in shop and bus,
Their clammy, cold, diseases,
So companies can sell to us
Their remedies for sneezes.

Thinking

There's never a ban on thinking,
All that's required is a brain.
It's free and as easy as blinking,
You can do it again and again.
It's healthy, and done by the best,
It may be, and can be, quite fun.
Then why does my research suggest,
That it's something that's so rarely done?

The Mysteries of Life

God called us all up together
To give us the latest brief
On life, and death, and that sort of thing,
But I got bored, and fell asleep.

At the end, after questions were dealt with,
And folk all prepared to depart,
I grunted, snorted, and my elbow slipped,
Waking me up with a start.

I put up my hand without thinking, and asked:
Hey, God, what's life all about?
God's noble face contorted with rage
As He answered, with an Almighty shout:

While I've been explaining the Mysteries of Life,
You chose to doze off and snore!
Now go, and forever stay out of my sight!
I never learnt any more.

For He sent me away with a flea in my ear
Which buzzes, and causes me pain.
It disturbs me and gives me a vague sense of fear,
And I've never been near God again.

The Emperor of Pluto

I'm the Emperor of Pluto,
And I've come back down to Earth,
To pay a friendly visit
To the planet of my birth.

In 'Situations Vacant',
Many years ago,
I saw the job being advertised
And thought *I've got to go!*

I cycled off to Pluto,
It took me quite a while.
They interviewed me straight away
Then sat back with a smile:

You're just the type we're looking for:
Imaginative and smart!
You've self-belief, which rulers need:
How quickly can you start?

Since that day, I've ruled them all:
The planet, with its army.
And now I've come back down to Earth,
Please don't say I'm barmy.

Knockin' on Heaven's Door

An MP went to heaven
On account of being dead,
Knocked upon The Pearly Gates,
With confidence, he said:
Hey! St. Peter! Let me in!
The rules say that you should!
I've worked so hard in Parliament –
All for the public good!
How shocked he was, when,
From inside, St Peter gave a yell:
This is just your second home!
Your main one's down in Hell!

Things to ignore

A fly-ridden child on the evening news
A cider'd tramp in an afternoon snooze
The morning dosser with hand held high
Who hurries your step as you scurry on by.

Its not, of course, that you never cared
It's more the way that you're easily scared
By the closeness of the debris of haphazard luck
To the rickety structure that keeps you up.

View by Appointment

This one's just come on the market:
the owner's decided to sell.
We're sure when you see it you'll like it:
- a biosphere in its own shell!

Kept at a comfortable temperature
by a safe, convenient sun,
it's a great place for work, or adventure,
to relax, or just to have fun!

Oceans and forests are features,
as are mountains, deserts, and lakes,
with a stunning selection of creatures –
birds, fish, mammals and snakes!

It has masses of water, and space to explore -
there's even an orbiting moon!
Buyers are beating a path to our door,
best put in a bid very soon!

It's a property exceedingly pleasant,
with aspects to please everyone.
Yes, it has tenants at present,
…but we're certain they'll soon be gone.

Just the Job

Genghis Khan is cleaning my loo,
It's the sort of job that he loves to do.
Our drains were cleared out by Attila the Hun,
Sewers and stench pipes are his kind of fun.
At unblocking the sink I was a failure,
And so I rang up Vlad the Impaler.
When our dog had diarrhoea it caused such distress,
Until Ivan the Terrible cleared up the mess.
If you want dirty jobs done without fuss,
Then I'd recommend "Tyrants 'R' Us".

Fly

The fly rests on the tablecloth
Too near my lunchtime snack.
I raise my arm with steadied wrath,
To give a fatal smack.

I poise my hand and concentrate
Then swiftly let it drop.
The fly speeds off - I'm just too late,
And slap the table-top.

Dear fly, unscathed, you thrive anew,
So swiftly did you flee.
I hope that I'm as fast as you
When the Big Hand comes for me.

Cockney Farmers

Cockney farmers softly toil
to get the best from London soil.
They plough in strips all down the Strand,
sow barley on that fertile land.
Rotate their crops in Rotherhythe,
whilst Hackney's left as set aside.

Cockney farmers claim to sow
their finest crops in soil from Bow
and moan that land in Spitalfields
produces only moderate yields.
At summer's end they all help lay
out hayricks made from Lambeth hay.

Cockney farmers fiercely dream
of grazing sheep on Bethnal Green.
They drive their cows from Tower Hill
down to the Thames to sup their fill.
And under cover of friendly dark
they loose their pigs in Regent's Park.

All tourists in the London crowd,
where all is garish, fast and loud,
should not fear to feel a nudge
from earthy plough or sense the trudge
or smell the smell or hear the sound
of cockney farmers breaking ground.

My Uncle's Bum

My Uncle's Bum! was what
my grandma used to say,
in times of stress or disbelief,
when nothing went her way.

It never caught on as a saying,
but later, I was told,
the behind my grandma referred to
was truly a sight to behold.

It belonged, indeed, to an uncle,
who was caught with a landowner's wife,
and, faced with a big barrelled shotgun,
was forced to flee for his life.

Bare–bottomed, he shot out the bedroom
and started his homeward run
when a blast of lead from the weapon
scattered all over his bum.

He escaped with his life, but the scars remained
right 'til the day he was dead.
He'd show his backside, as a party piece,
all pock-marked, mottled, and red.

So famous it was, he got took on
by a number of travelling shows.
It even got seen by the King and his Queen,
...or so the story goes.

New Prayer

I'd love it if there were a God
Oh yes, I really would.
A promised land where angels trod
Why, then I would be good.

And how much simpler, too, to know
There really was a hell.
For then I'd really have a go
At not being bad, as well.

Fishy

Every day fish come ashore
to buy things for their tea.
They fill their shopping bags with food
and then go back to sea.
They make their dripping way through town
at exactly half past three.
Hooked on little bargains like:
Buy one, get one free!
Queuing in the Co-op,
they're not that hard to see.
Then why do they remain unseen
by everyone but me?

Tiffany Winters

Tiffany Winters hits the scene,
Dark eyes flicker like a video screen.
Fists clenched tight, mouth turned down,
Tiffany Winters comes to town.

Pale-faced waif, small but hard,
She can outrun any security guard.
Her clothes are hot, but always cool:
Tiffany Winters is nobody's fool.

Of teachers, Tiffany has no fear,
For she's not been near her school for a year.
She learns her lessons out on the street,
Where the quick and the crooked make ends meet.

Tiffany Winters has a bloody mind,
Lives in a flat that's hard to find.
In a grim estate of disillusion,
Where no-one's heard of social inclusion.

She's never, ever, seen her dad,
And her mother's boyfriends drive her mad.
The police turn up, from time to time,
While Tiffany Winters turns to crime.

Her social worker closed the case
And left the job without being replaced.
Awkward questions remain unasked
While Tiffany Winters grows up fast.

In the local church, the vicar prays
For wicked sinners to mend their ways.
While outside, Tiffany hangs round bars,
And sells herself in the backs of cars.

But God, in his own mysterious way,
Cares for Tiffany, still, they say.
And what does Tiffany think, in return?
God, she thinks, has a lot to learn.

Paddle Creek

I went to Paddle Creek,
Where people seldom go.
And looked down in the deep,
And watched the water flow.

Down there at the bottom,
On the murky, muddy floor,
Slowly going rotten,
Were paddles by the score.

Nearby is another creek,
From where each paddle came,
Where many folk have come to grief:
I'm sure you know its name.

Getting On

Hair thins out
with passing years,
More will sprout
from nose and ears.
Horizons dwindle,
waistlines spread,
Sleep is all
we do in bed.
We ought to diet,
days are boring.
Nights are quiet,
except for snoring…

My Cat

My cat enjoys playing with mice.
He joins in their card games at night.
They fleece him at pontoon and poker.
He can't seem to play his cards right.

Raiding the fridge, he'll pull out some cheese
He says that he'll win back some more.
But early next morning, with nowt in his paws
He's howling outside at the door.

Why don't you give up? I ask him
You know, you haven't a clue!
Those mice only want you because of your cheese-
They're far too smart for you!

Once, he used to play with frogs
And lose to them at pool.
They'd snigger each time he missed a shot.
The way that they'd mock him was cruel.

He'd play with birds, at off-ground tig.
They'd laugh and go *Tweet, tweet.*
And when he'd clamber up on a twig
They'd fly away, twittering *Cheat!*

Now, every night, he'll take some cheese
To join in the mice's school.
He never wins, he never will:
My cat is just a fool.

The Jibber Jabber Tree

The Jibber Jabber Tree talks nonsense,
Spouts it all day long,
Until it reaches evening,
When it sings a nonsense song.

Yet few have heard it talk or sing,
For it's also very shy,
And goes completely silent
If anyone's nearby.

So, if you want to hear it,
Be wary, on your guard:
Learn to keep your distance,
And listen, very hard.

Surreal to Real

Giant, drug-crazed, blue bananas
marching across the volcanic sky,
spitting life-sized glass piranhas
at bowler-hatted passers-by.
Giraffes in cages, made of butter,
paying firemen riding deer
to walk their lobsters in the gutter:
none of these are welcome here.
Instead, I'll recall the garden in summer
where I sat and smiled in mild alarm
as a bee landed on me, gently humming,
looking for nectar in the hairs on my arm.

Erik the Cabbage

Eric was a cabbage.
Which wasn't to his liking.
He wanted to be savage
- a fierce and scary Viking!

He got himself a helmet
to try and look more mean,
and set off in a longboat
to join the Viking scene.

When the Vikings saw him
they all knew what to do.
They hacked and chopped and boiled him
to make a cabbage stew.

The moral of this story?
There's not one I'm afraid.
Except, if you're a cabbage,
don't join a Viking raid.

Second Coming

A drunkard sees, on Christmas Eve,
Angels round a wheelie bin.
He staggers close, and thinks he hears
Crying from within.

He lifts the lid and looks inside,
At a large black plastic sack.
Nestling with some rubbish,
A baby smiles back.

Sobered now, he lifts the child,
Decides to take it to
Somewhere where they'll be someone
Who might know what to do.

The nearest place is hospital,
He thinks that would be best.
He takes it to reception,
And lays it on the desk.

A nurse looks up, suspiciously.
And what is wrong with him?
Nothing, said the man, *Except-*
I found him in a bin

Security! the nurse calls out,
A uniform strolls in,
And frowns to learn a baby's here,
Fresh from a wheelie bin.

We had three blokes, quite wealthy ones,
All looking for a child!
Then farmers came, with animals-
It drove the cleaners wild!

And now, there's this, an abandoned kid!
There's something up, no doubt!
Best ring social services,
They can sort it out!

There's more to this than meets the eye!
The nurse on duty sighs.
God moves in mysterious ways!
The Christmas drunk replies.

The baby boy stays smiling.
He lies there, watching all.
And gives a look as if to say
He's been through this before.

Outside

The day we went outside...

there were no signs to guide us by;
just distance, space, and tall, wide sky.
No walls, or doors with numbers on -
just open land, with boundaries gone.

The day we went outside...

there was no fridge or freezer there;
just food that grew, and lived, in air.
No baths or kettles, oozing steam -
we washed and drank in a cool, clear, stream.

The day we went outside....

there was no TV, video, phone;
just us, each other, all alone.
No lights, no room, no cosy bed -
at night, just stars, and dark, instead.

The day we went outside....

we cried...
to think of all we'd never tried
while safe and warm and kept inside.

R.E.

He seldom ever went to church
and never Sunday school.
Even, as a little boy,
he knew it wasn't cool.
He's never since felt at a loss
because he couldn't say
why some folk like to wear a cross
or why, on Xmas day,
the baby Jesus came to light
behind some stable doors -
the mum, he's sure, was Mary,
and the father, Santa Claus.
Also, he can't fathom out
why, every Eastertide,
we celebrate the sad fact that
the Easter bunny died.

The Weather Boy

The weather boy breezes outside in the morning,
Shakes all the trees and makes the leaves fall.
Whirls down the pavements and swirls up the puddles,
Storms by his playmates, drenching them all.

A lightning dash across the field,
Startling the crows and scattering rooks,
The weather boy thunders his way into school,
Rattling the windows and clattering books.

Morning arithmetic slows him down;
The outlook is gloomy, the weather boy's glum.
Long division, and multiplication,
A fog descends as he ponders a sum.

Time for lunch, his stomach is rumbling,
Teachers look anxiously out at the sky.
The weather boy munches on tornado dumplings,
With hurricane beans and hailstone pie.

Nicely filled up, the weather boy brightens,
Grey morning clouds all faded away.
The sun's soft glow embraces the school,
The weather boy beams, and warms to the day.

The final bell rings – the school day is ended;
The weather boy wonders, where time has flown.
Giving his teacher a heatwave goodbye,
He puffs out his cheeks, to blow himself home.

Beyond the school gates, parents are waiting.
Seeing him coming, they patiently sigh.
Bracing themselves, they hold fast their hats,
Wrap their coats tighter until he's rushed by.

A busy day closes, and darkness descends;
The night sky twinkles, glitters, and gleams.
A cushion of stars watch from above,
And wink to the echo of the weather boy's dreams.

Zombies by the seaside

Zombies by the seaside,
see them rush and shout!
Fooling round with seaweed,
kicking sand about!

Zombies by the seaside,
splashing in the waves!
Aggravating bathers,
they should be home in graves.

Zombies by the seaside,
peeling in the sun.
Scaring dogs and cats and kids
is their idea of fun.

Zombies by the seaside
stagger down the pier.
They've sold their worms to anglers
and used the cash for beer.

Zombies by the seaside,
all beach attendants dread
collecting fees for sunbeds
from the rows of living dead.

Zombies by the seaside
sit and watch the tide,
exactly like we used to
in the days before we died.

Note about the author.

When he was a child, Martin Brown was abducted by aliens.
Almost immediately, a group of space marines
were sent to snatch him back.
They succeeded.
Undeterred, the aliens abducted him once more.
And so on.
This to-ing and fro-ing went on for years,
with the result that Martin now regards himself
as equally at home both on Earth
and on the planet Zibblesnox,
with friends, magazine subscriptions,
and a spare pair of underpants on both planets.

Shake, Rattle & Custard
by Martin Brown
Published by Pressbutton Press
(c) 2010
ISBN 978-0-9566584-0-1